Prairie Sketches

Kansas Life & Lore

Prairie Sketches

Kansas Life & Lore

Raymond S. Nelson

Art work by
Stan Nelson

Hearth

Hearth Publishing Company
Hillsboro, Kansas

TABLE OF CONTENTS

NATURE'S QUIRKS

LAW AND DISORDER

RESTLESS TIMES

POLITICAL VIGNETTES

ARTISTS IN RESIDENCE

LIST OF ILLUSTRATIONS

POETRY

No simple definition of poetry is possible. There are many kinds of poetry: epic, lyric, narrative, dramatic, satiric, to name just a few, and no one definition gets us very far. Even fashions vary in poetry from age to age so that it is difficult to say that poetry is "measured language" or that it usually assumes some form of verse. We are living in an age wherein most celebrated artists have rejected traditional forms and devices. Yet most poets and critics would agree, I think, that poetry communicates indirectly through images of sight, sound, touch, taste, or smell. Beyond that, we have to consider the type of poetry and the many traditions.

In my lyric poetry I try to express feelings and thoughts that are interrelated. Somehow ideas and images combine or express emotion, and the combination of all three produces pleasure (and profit). I try to compress the ideas into brief space. I use everyday words whenever possible. I express many ideas obliquely. I use normal English syntax. And of course I seek to use images appropriate to the subject matter and to my purposes. These are my guidelines.

In my narrative poetry I use the same guidelines: everyday words, some obliqueness, regular English syntax, appropriate images, and a blend of thought with emotion. But narrative poetry requires a story line, and narrative poems tend to be longer than lyric poems. The narrative line then often substitutes for "images" in that the story itself becomes an image or symbol.

Distinctions among genres of poetry are not absolute. One genre flows into another freely, so that some narratives have lyric qualities and many lyric poems imply actions. That is perhaps why a quality that seems to flow through all of our classifications nevertheless makes them poetry.

THE COSMIC DANCE

Icecaps melt and icecaps grow;
Earthquakes rend the face of earth;
Volcanic lava burns all things;
Cyclonic winds lash out to strow
The earth with trash. But soon rebirth
Occurs: from rubble order springs.
    Nothing stays the same.

Ancient forests long since stone;
Seaborn fossils found on high;
Mammoth bones on rolling plains;
Forgotten towns long overgrown
And fabled empires lost to eye
Speak loud of shifts no one explains.
    Nothing stays the same.

Nations live and nations die;
Systems work and systems fail
In faith and polity and war;
Armies fight and armies fly,
Statesmen seek a stable vale
While borders change and ruffians roar.
    Nothing stays the same.

Midwestern plains were once a sea,
Then glaciers ground across the land.
Dinosaurs and mammoths ranged
Where later buffalo roamed free.
We cannot stay Dame Nature's hand;
We can at best concede what's changed.
    Nothing stays the same.

1

Stars are born each day, and die;
Oak trees topple, acorns sprout;
Raging rivers gouge their banks;
Scorching winds make sand to fly
In brand new deserts caused by drought—
All rounds of Nature's endless dance.
              Nothing stays the same.

BLIZZARD

The snow began one January day,
Jim, in eighteen eighty-six. I'd say
About mid-afternoon. The air was chill
—Near zero—and I noticed that the mill was still.
The snow lay smooth and deep
Before I finished chores and went to sleep.

At dawn I heard a moaning wind, a sound
Just like a distant wailing train, and found
I could not open up my door. A drift
Reached almost to the eaves, but I could lift
A window on the other side. The sky
Was gray. The swirling, blinding snow swept by.

I slipped out through the window to the shed
To tend the cows. I held a line that led
Back home if I should lose my way. I knew
The deadly hazard, yet the beasts, though few,
Must be watered, fed, and milked. I went
And came through blinding whiteness, almost spent.

All day it stormed, and then again, all night.
The second day was dark at noon, the light
Obscured by clouds of snow. Since fuel was low,
We went to bed for warmth. We melted snow
For water, just to see it freeze in pans
Between the fire and the cold's advance.

All night again the blizzard raged, but morning
Saw a slowing of the wind. The dawning
Was brighter, though the mercury read twenty-
Five below. By noon I knew that plenty
Now remained for Meg and me to do
For livestock, household needs—and neighbors too.

Blizzard

It was an alien world. We looked in vain
For fences, buildings, shrubs, and stacks. The plain
Looked like a rolling sea, an endless sea
Of waves with househigh drifts. A nearby tree
Was visible to break the wasteland white
That stretched in all directions out of sight.

The steers on open range were on their own.
The drifts and cold and wind kept us at home,
With hopes they'd find the scattered stacks of hay
Though partly buried by the snow. No way.
We found weeks later most had died. We bent
Beneath that staggering loss, our spirits spent.

A neighbor lost his eldest son. His wife
Went mad with grief. We suffered much, but life
Seemed good, despite the loss. Then springtime came
To call us to another year, our aim
To look ahead though gloom and shade pervade
The mem'ries clinging to each desperate day.

THE PLAGUE

It happened here in Kansas late
In eighteen seventy-four. The wheat,
Thank God, was in across the state.
The summer, though, was incomplete.

I'll tell you how it was, Maureen.
You'll never quite believe it, though,
For it was like a troubled dream.
They came in clouds that drifted slow

From out the west and north, to fall
Like silver snowflakes on the land.
I heard a droning hum that all
But made me think of Gramma and

Her spinning wheel. They made the sun
Go dim, yet sun rays glinted on
Their filmy wings. They seemed to come
And come and come. All hope seemed gone.

They settled on all growing things—
On corn and grass and vines and trees—
Crawling on with folded wings,
And stripped all greenery with ease.

The ground was covered with a layer
Four inches thick at times, a mass
Of wriggling life, enough to scare
The strongest man or halest lass.

The hoppers nibbled on my clothes.
They ate the wool right off some sheep
And chewed the handles on our hoes,
Day and night, awake, asleep,

The horde was there, and we felt through.
We beat them, burned them, plowed them, true,
But nothing helped. We were so few
And knew of nothing else to do.

A thousand thousand jaws chewed on,
The sound a muted buzz-saw hum,
Incessant grinding, on and on.
The raiding horde left not a crumb.

A faintly fetid odor filled
The air. The wells were fouled, the water
Stank. We carried on, we willed
To overcome, my son and daughter,

Husband Tom and I. They stayed
A week, then left as they had come,
To leave the farm as if a raid
Had stripped us. We felt quite undone.

Threatening Sky

AFTER THE STORM

I'd seen pictures of storm damage, Tim,
But never anything like this. The trees
Were twisted off like matchsticks, and John's house
Was leaning crazily. The power lines
Lay all across the pavement, blocking cars
And trucks till linemen had a chance to clear
The street. I could hardly take it in.
His yard was shoulder deep in rubble—sticks
And paper, corrugated metal sheets
From a shop across the way, branches, boards,
Shingles, boxes, even clothing from
Some woman's lines. Someone's mobile home
Lay upside down in Johnny's yard, in back.
The wind had carried it a block or two
And dropped it there. I saw some men with rakes
And saws and trailers ready to begin
The overwhelming job of cleaning up.
Others stood in knots, uncertain what
To think or say. I'd seen pictures on
T.V. and in the paper, just like you,
But never really understood how bad
It was. I never will forget that sight.

DUSTSTORM

I couldn't even see the road, Laree.
The cloud of dirt was black as night,
So I pulled off to the side and stopped. But when
The dust cleared some, and I could partly see,
I saw a car just feet ahead. The sight
Upset me so I feared to drive again.

That night I stayed in Tribune with a friend—
It was in 'thirty-four, I think—we shut
The windows and the doors despite the heat.
We even sealed the cracks, but dust did tend
To sift in anyway. I washed up, but
In minutes felt fresh grime and knew defeat.

The lights shone dimly in the dining room
Where we sat down to eat. A brownish haze
Suffused the air. We lightly joked at first
About our failing sight, but soon the gloom
Oppressed our spirits. Thinking of the day's
Half night, I longed to see the dark dispersed.

I sweltered in my bed that night, but slept
Till early dawn. My pillowcase was brown
With dust—except the place my head had been.
It filtered everywhere. I even kept
My clothes in bags. The dust motes settled down
On everything, you see, to my chagrin.

The ditches filled with sifting dust as deep
As winter snow. It covered fences, spoiled
The fields and crops as topsoil blew away.
The drouth combined with ceaseless wind to keep
Dark clouds on high, while desperate farmers toiled
With little hope till rain should come some day.

BAT MASTERSON

Bat Masterson was born in 1853 to a fairly large family of boys. Henry Raymond, friend of the Masterson family, kept a diary in which he commented on the boys from time to time, sometimes in careful detail. Details of Bat's early life are few—fragmentary throughout—but some facts are pretty well known. He fought in the battle of Adobe Walls on June 27, 1874. It was a fairly matched battle, apparently. But with each retelling of the story by raconteurs and newsmen, there were fewer and fewer white men and more and more Indians. In November of 1877 Bat was elected sheriff of Ford County, assuming office on January 14, 1878. His territory, however, comprised thirteen other unincorporated counties in the region, a huge area. An early challenge came Bat's way when six men attempted to rob a Santa Fe Railroad train on January 27, 1878, at Kinsley, Kansas, thirty miles away from Dodge City, Bat's headquarters. The robbers scattered, and Bat formed a posse to chase—and catch—two of them. Some months later, he captured two more. His days were filled with problems caused by boisterous Texas cowboys, killers, horse thieves, con men, drunks, and so on, not made any easier by criticism that began to develop from various Kansas newspaper editors and writers as his administration continued. After two years he was not re-elected, though he continued to travel in and out of Dodge City until the 1890's.

When Bat turned from law enforcement,he took up sports, then developed interests in silver mining speculation in Trinidad, Colorado, and later managed an Athletic Club in Denver. During these days it became evident that he could write well, even describe a horse race in process. He married Emma Walters in 1891, and continued to live in the West until the early twentieth century. Late in life he moved to New York where he became a sports writer for the *Morning Telegraph*. He died at his desk on October 25, 1921.

BAT MASTERSON

I knew Bat better than most men.
We used to hunt together. Then
We went our separate ways, and news
Of him came through reporters' views
And family visits and rare lines.
He was a scout and knew the signs
Of Indians like his own bronzed hand
And led our troops across the land
He'd come to know so well. One day
He rode with hunters on their way
To southern herds when Cheyenne braves
Attacked. As Indians came in waves
The hunters sought Adobe Walls,
A trading post nearby. Close calls
Aplenty came, but only three
Whites died. Bat later went to see
The Indian toll, and counted ten.
The battle done, the battered men
Rode out, this time to Dodge. There Bat
Tied his horse and hung his hat.
Bat was a slender man those years,
Five-nine in stocking feet, no fears
Apparent in his clear blue eyes
Or bearing. Many felt surprise
That such a dapper gentleman
Would turn a lawman when he ran
For sheriff. Only twenty-five,
Tough, and very much alive,
He thrived. He set his standards high
In service, confident to try
His skill. Installed scarce thirteen days
In office, Bat set out to raise
A trace of six train robbers (ten
At first were thought the number), men

Who tried to rob a train nearby
In Kinsley. Knowing every eye
Was on him, Bat appointed three
Good men to ride with him to tree
The fugitives from justice. Luck
was with them. Four days out they struck
A trail and caught Dave Ruddabaugh
And Edward West. With two in tow,
Bat stayed in Dodge to keep the peace;
His duties never seemed to cease
From herding cowboys, jailing drunks,
To watching gamblers, queans, and punks.
When two months passed, word came on down
That four train robbers were in town,
Sizing up the scene. Bat sent
For help, then moving swiftly went
To southern Dodge where soon he saw
Two rascal renegades—not four.
With little trouble, soon the other two
Were lodged in jail, but not a clue
Could Bat find of the rest. Yet four
Of six is quite a passing score.
Dodge City saw his wit and strength
And courage, chasing men the length
And breadth of thirteen counties—horse
Thieves, con men, killers—source
Of frontier violence and crime.
He killed some men, though in his time
The legends far outran the truth.
No matter. Legends bolstered youth.
He used a golden headed cane
As much as pulled a gun to gain
His ends. Wild stories floated far
And wide of the man who wore the star.
Young Bat was feared on every side.

Just two years more and parties vied
To vote him out, and did. He turned
To politics and sports. He earned
New spurs in Colorado towns
Though Dodge remained his special ground.
His skill in writing brought new fame
And new career. His household name,
Made famous by the *New York Sun*,
Saw Bat a newsman, laurels won,
Grown old in honor, ever with the law,
A frontier legend, widely held in awe.

THE DALTON GANG

James Lewis Dalton married Adeline Younger in 1851, and together they had fifteen children—ten boys and five girls. Franklin Dalton was a respected U. S. deputy marshal who lost his life trying to arrest whiskey runners in Arkansas. Three of the boys (Gratton, Robert, and Emmett) were outlaws for about two years before their death on October 6, 1892, though all three had served as lawmen some years before they turned to crime. Mason (Bill) Dalton also became an outlaw shortly after the Coffeyville fiasco, and was killed by a posse in June of 1894. A museum exists in Coffeyville to memorialize the abortive bank holdups. The rest of the family were law abiding citizens, though it is probable that some of them gave aid and refuge to their brothers on separate occasions.

Eva Dalton Whipple lived for a while in Meade, Kansas, during the late 1880's in the house now made into a museum. The house is connected by a tunnel to a barn about one hundred feet away, and it is generally believed that her brothers and other outlaws sometimes rode into the barn, slipped undetected through the tunnel to the house, to remain quite secure while neighbors were unaware of their presence.

The Dalton Gang began their career in crime with a series of train robberies, actual or attempted, in California. The newspapers told all such stories in exaggerated detail, of course, and before long almost all train and bank robberies in the west were attributed to the Dalton Gang. As the heat of pursuit became intense, the gang rode east to the Cimarron River, which became the staging place for their disastrous attempt on the Coffeyville banks.

LAST RAID OF THE DALTONS

"The Daltons are robbing the banks" came the cry
From Charles Gump in the middle of town.
"Shut up, said old Billy, "or you'll surely die,"
And he lectured the lad with a frown.

"Don't trifle with Daltons," he said to the lad,
"They're poison you want to avoid.
They've been robbing and shooting, they've gone to the bad,
And there's dozens that want them destroyed."

One lawman alone had followed the gang
For hundreds of miles on the trail.
He pressed on their heels as news accounts rang
Of the exploits he could not curtail.

And now they were here. It seemed perfectly clear
They had plans that might render great harm.
To dare to give warning, not cower in fear,
Led the lad to cry out his alarm.

The Daltons had trotted on down the main street
The dust swirling up round their horses,
But found that all hitching posts lay at their feet—
They were driven to other resources.

The city was putting board sidewalks in place,
And buildings had changed since the boys
Had lived there. They hurriedly chose a new base
In an alley nearby for their ploys.

Leaving their mounts, the five men strode out
With winchesters loose at their side.
Three entered one bank, and just then the shout
That I mentioned rang out far and wide.

The three in the Condon Bank led by young Grat
Gave orders to fill up a sack,
But banker Charles Ball delayed the main act
Pretending the time-lock set back.

"We'll wait," said the bandit, "though not very long,"
As he anxiously peered through the glass.
"I wonder how Emmett and Bob have got on,"
He said as he watched some men pass.

The others had entered the National Bank
And loaded a sack with some coin.
But the shouts had been heard, and nobody shrank
From agreeing resistance to join.

By then men had hurried for guns left at home
And others for guns in a store.
They started to shoot, intending to comb
Every corner, each window and door.

Their plans all awry, the bandits lit out,
Though dragging two sacks filled with loot.
They shot as they ran a zigzagging route
With the townsmen in earnest pursuit.

Each shot at the other, and several fell,
The air filled with lead and with smoke.
They ran to the alley with hopes to repel
The resisters with masterful stroke.

But Gratton was hit. He tumbled face down,
And Bill Powers fell to the ground.
Not long after, Bob fell with a frown,
And Emmett took mount with a bound.

He started away, but returned for young Bob,
An error as sure as the day,
For a volley of buckshot finished the job
And Emmett fell limp on the clay.

Emmett was battered, but he didn't die.
The tally was heavy each side.
Four citizens dead, four bandits to tie,
With others sore wounded beside.

This saga of Coffeyville lives with her name,
Her citizens brought her great fame.
The populace gathered in thanks to acclaim
The heroes who saw the gang slain.

CARRY A. NATION

Carry Nation was born on November 25, 1846, in Kentucky. She married Dr. Charles Gloyd, a physician, in November of 1867 only to discover on her wedding day that he was an alcoholic. One child, Charlien, was born to this marriage. Carry left Dr. Gloyd after only a year or so, and he died six months later from dissipation.

In 1877 she married David Nation, attorney, minister, and editor. He was improvident, and the second marriage was as unhappy as the first had been, though for different reasons.

Forced to make a living, Carry ran a series of hotels as she moved from city to city. In this way she supported several dependents. But she was also deeply religious in her fiercely pietistic manner. She was outspoken in worship services, critical of most churches and ministers, and violently self-reliant. The Bible was a fetish to her. She carried it always, though she often spoke abusively to those who opposed her. "Stated loosely," Robert Lewis Taylor says, "Mrs. Nation was against alcohol, tobacco, sex, politics, government (national, state and local), the Masonic Lodge, William McKinley, Theodore Roosevelt and William Jennings Bryan, in approximately that order."

In her fifty-fourth year she decided that saloons ("joints" she called them) were the greatest destroyers of men and families. She went from Medicine Lodge, her home, to Kiowa and smashed three joints while singing "Peace on Earth, Good Will to Men," and a variety of anti-liquor songs. She felt justified in her violence because Kansas was technically a dry state, and joints were illegal. The law was not enforced. Two days after Christmas in 1900 she came to Wichita, and smashed more saloons. She wound up in jail, and thereafter for the next decade, she smashed saloons and went to jail routinely. At first she used rocks and brickbats to smash mirrors, windows and bottles, but soon turned to a hatchet as her favorite tool of destruction. She became an instant national figure after the Wichita affair.

Carry Nation also hated tobacco. She was allergic to smoke. She abused smokers, snatching cigarettes and cigars from smokers' mouths.

Yet many knew her as a kindly, motherly person. She was generous and helpful to people in need. She kept virtually no money for herself, but used all of her resources for her program.

Violent, bigoted, unreasonable, tunnel-visioned, she was not insane. In a day when women did not have votes and had no political power, she did what she could to confront what were to her major problems.

Carry Nation

THE SMASHER

With Kiowa behind her, Carry Nation
Soon had schemes and plans in preparation
For the joints in Wichita. She spent
A night in prayer before she packed and went
Aboard the Santa Fe to make her way
To the City of Sin. She'd find a place to stay
Then look around. She wanted to survey
The scene before she acted out her part.
She chose a room, then with a mother's heart
She cruised from joint to joint—fourteen in all—
And warned of retribution soon to fall.
Saloons were wrecking lives and homes, she thought;
Besides, they were against the law and ought
Not be! Her round almost complete, she meant
To go back to her room for rest, but bent
Her steps to one last place, the Carey Bar.
She glanced inside, recoiling with a jar,
To see a painting fastened to the wall,
Called "Cleopatra at Her Bath"! A squall
Broke at the sight. She shrieked an "Aie!" then raced
Away to fret and stew. She paced and paced
Her room (the man below got little sleep
That night). At dawn she settled down to keep
Her date with destiny. She dressed in black
Alpaca, dark poke bonnet, at her neck
A neat white bow. She tied an iron rod
And ring to a heavy cane before she trod
Into the street for smooth white stones. By eight
O'clock she sailed (A Man of War) straight
To Carey's Bar, the finest in the West.
The polished cherry wood, John Noble's best
Art work reflected in the mirror, rails
Of brass, cut glass decanters—all were scales
Of luxury provided in this haven

21

Sought by drouthy men in search of Eden.
Carry stepped across the threshold, lips
Pressed tight beneath her pug nose, whitened tips
Of fingers grasping stones. She let one fly
At naked Cleopatra, turned to try
Her luck with mirrored nudity. The glass
Fell in a thousand fragments. Men en masse
Fled from this whirling cyclone. Picking up
Her armored cane, she swept each glass and cup
From off the shelves along the wall. She beat
The polished cherry bar; she sought complete
Destruction, striking chandeliers and brass
Spittoons, doors and windows, making pass
After pass at treasures. Bartender Pauley hid
Behind the bar. People soon were bid
To gather by the scattered men and noise,
And they gathered by the hundreds, men and boys.
The cry, "Help, Police," brought a man of law.
He took her by the arm, but then he saw
The swinging cane and ducked. "I arrest
You, Ma'am," he said. "Me?" she cried, "The beast
That runs this hole should be your prisoner."
Park Massey took the cane away, and her
As well. He brought her to the jail, the first
Of many times. Like Joan of Arc, she burst
The bands of custom and propriety
And paid the price that difference decrees.
A feisty lady with a heart of gold,
Carry Nation blithely broke the mold—
A reformer of whom endless tales are told!

CHEYENNES RETURN

"Going Home" is based on Mari Sandoz' *Cheyenne Autumn*, that classic American epic. The novel and the poem are based on real people and actual events. Little Wolf and Dull Knife did indeed lead a band of Cheyennes from the banks of the North Canadian River in what was then Indian Territory (Oklahoma) to the banks of the Yellowstone River in Montana. It happened in 1878-79. They traveled then northward through Oklahoma, Kansas, Nebraska, and on to their traditional grounds. They left with 283 persons and ended with 114. Ironically, after all the resistance by whites, and extensive suffering and loss by Indians, the Tongue River Reservation was established in Montana.

The Northern Cheyennes had been persuaded early in 1877 by Indian Agency officials to go south with promises of food and provisions, plus the assurance that they could return home if they were not satisfied. But, as almost always, the whites (referred to as *vehos* by the Indians) did not keep their word. There was no food for the Indians in Oklahoma. There were no supplies. There was no intention to allow the Cheyennes to return to Montana. In desperation then, ragged and famished, the Indians unilaterally took up the option that had been promised: they went home.

Although Little Wolf was an exceptionally good leader, he had difficulty restraining some of the "dog soldiers" in his charge. They committed outrages along the way—several rapes of women and children as well as the wanton killing of men and animals. No excuse can be offered for such actions, but they can be understood as expressions of pent up frustration and rage that had built up over many months. Young extremists behave rather much the same among all peoples at all times.

Little Wolf lost his position as chief in Montana after he killed Little Elk, a fellow tribesman, but he lived on for another twenty-five years in private life, a genuine friend to several whites, most notably Nannie Alderson, who said of him, he had "a quiet resignation to the inevitableness of things" as well as "integrity and inner peace."

Chief Little Wolf Late in Life

GOING HOME

A silent stirring marked the moonlit night
As warriors, wives and children softly crept
From cone shaped lodges in their purposed flight
To northern plains, a plan each one had kept
In secret from the soldiers who now slept
Nearby. They drifted like the mist or smoke
Across the plain without dark night as cloak.

The moon shone bright upon the treeless plain,
No cloud to help conceal the stealthy forms
That bent like grazing bison to attain
Their ends—no alarm must trigger swarms
Of men to swoop upon the tribe with storms
Of cannon shells, of musket fire, or sword.
The risk was great, but so was the reward.

These Cheyennes from the North had come far south
At point of gun. Now, with idle hands
And broken promises, with empty mouth
And nagging hunger, threats they must to lands
Yet farther on, the tribesmen took two stands:
They would resist and would in honor trace
Their steps to ancient timeworn ways and space.

The Great Father's men had promised food
And clothes long months ago. "Go south," they said,
"Without your guns. We'll feed and clothe you. Should
You need a thing, you'll get it there." Instead,
The Indians got no food, no clothes, no bed,
No robes, and now were being forced to go
Still far beyond the North Canadian's flow.

Time had run out. Next dawn the tribe must go
Where soldiers led the way, unless the plan
Long since worked out could turn the tide. They know,
From young to old, that flight means—to a man—
The risk of death. Yet no one shrinks. From van
To rearguard, young and old, each person moves
In concert and the leadership approves.

Little Wolf, long chosen by the men
In council, was their leader in this break
For freedom. Long ago and now again,
Knowing fury and restraint, he'd take
The burden of the Sacred Arrows, make
The welfare of the tribe his central goal
And pray the Powers daily for the whole.

Dull Knife's childhood name was Morning Star,
Now a chief for many years. He long
Had worked for peace, though many a livid scar
Revealed his prowess, while the women's Song
Of Celebration told of actions strong
And brave for forty years. He was a man
Revered at home and feared in rival clan.

Chiefs Little Wolf and Dull Knife led the way
While warriors stole near the army guard
To silence them should accident betray
The secret mass withdrawal from the yard
Prescribed by whites. But no mischance marred
The Council's plan of action. People knew
Just where to go as well as what to do.

The rivulets of people slowly massed
Away from alien eyes. They carried gear
They'd need, and warriors with saddles passed
No chance to take a horse from soldiers near
Or settlers farther on the trail. The rear
Guard kept the stragglers moving on
So that the tribe was gathered in by dawn.

They knew the trail would soon be hot. They hurried
On, but scavenged freely for the days
To come. The company moved swiftly, scurried
Like a clutch of chicks. They knew the ways
Of scouts, but could not hide their trail, a blaze
They left behind. There was no time. They fled
As quarry, all intent to get ahead.

By early dawn the tribe had traveled miles
And came to rough terrain where they could hide,
Perchance find food. Ah, yes. Bison. Smiles
And nods, for all were famished. They decide
To kill, but hardly can before one cried,
"Soldiers coming! Quickly. Eat and run
Before they see us! Quickly. Let's have done."

The women took the meat and skins, and scattered
With the children out of sight. The men
Were spaced on hilltops far and wide, tattered
Troops from long neglect, but strong again
In spirit, ready to strike the bluecoats when
They came. But Little Wolf remained below
To parley with the fast approaching foe.

The soldiers slowed, then stopped to view the scene.
The Wolf, accompanied by Hog and Knife,
Walked slowly forward till they stood between.
The Wolf then strode alone to talk, his life
At risk, his only thought to forestall strife.
But nervous greenhorns, filled with fear and dread,
Attacked, and Wolf withdrew in a hail of lead.

The soldiers had more guns and better stock
But the Indians held the heights and fought with skill.
The warriors used each bit of brush and rock
To pill and plague the whites. By night the will
Of the soldiers waned and they withdrew. The hill
The Cheyennes held was free, though at a cost
To both in members wounded and men lost.

The soldiers camped that night, no water near
And ammunition low. At break of day
They struck their tents and gathered up their gear,
Returning to the fort. They cleared the way
For Little Wolf to rest, and then to say
To all: "We must hurry on. The road
Is long and we are weak, but yet unbowed."

Much work remained before the tribe moved out.
Some young men were sent for horses, some
Were charged with trailing whites, and some must scout
The trail ahead. Before the dawn should come
The Cheyenne must be gone, must leave no crumb
Behind. They looked for stragglers, for the few
Who'd had to hide, but now could rendezvous.

One woman had been hindered. She gave birth
Along the way, attended by a pair
Of women and some little ones. The earth
Was kind, affording a deep cave, a lair
For them to hide in. Brave One did not dare
To move too soon, but in good time she led
The party to the tribe. They were well sped.

Arrived in camp, the woman and her child
Required their due: he must have a name.
He shall be Comes Behind, his uncle smiled,
And waved his pipe before the Powers the same
Moment that he spoke. That done, no blame
Could be assigned. The rite was done despite
The hardships and the urgence of the flight.

The Cheyennes traveled north and slightly west
In ordered haste. They came in dead of night
To the Arkansas and its flooded crest,
A daunting bar in darkness or in light,
But, choosing a wide and shifting sandy site,
The young men planted willow poles to guide
The company across the torrent's tide.

Once safely over, everyone set out
For Punished Woman Creek. The canyons there
Held bison; and defense, without a doubt,
Was best at such a site. It could compare
With Turkey Springs, that first armed force affair,
For water, food, and rough terrain combined
To give advantage at each place assigned.

The Indians feasted, rested, knowing well
The time was short before their foes would come.
They set an ambush, sure their scouts would tell
When bluecoats neared. Two days went by, the sum
Of all things good. Then coyotes howled: the drum
Of distant hoofbeats marked the end of rest:
A clash was sure to prove a bitter test.

Chief Wolf was ready. "Keep from sight," he said.
"Let no man shoot until the soldiers ride
Well into the canyon. You'll be spread
To right and left above them. Let us bide
Our time." All agreed. The snare was tied,
The quarry lured by a trail still fresh and clear
Across the plain. The cavalry drew near.

The bluecoats rode in double file, a host
That Colonel Lewis led with colors high.
"We'll catch the tribe or die," he'd said in boast,
And hastened now into the trap. The sly
Old Wolf showed himself ahead, to try
To further tempt the soldiers to their fate.
They hurried on. They seemed to take the bait.

Then suddenly a shot rang out. A young
Cheyenne, too hot to wait as told, drew bead
And fired. The crafty, well-laid trap was sprung
And all advantage that surprise might breed
Was lost. The tide was turned. With lightning speed,
The soldiers whirled away in clouds of dust.
The Colonel then prepared his counterthrust.

He sent his men to circle round the tribe .
And shoot whoever came in view—a child,
A woman, or a man. He would ascribe
Such drastic action to subduing "wild
And wily savages," as he styled
His foes. The crossfire forced the Indians back
As men and horses died in the attack.

The bluecoats pressed the issue, hour by hour.
The Indians, plagued by scant supplies, slipped back
Until they could no more. The greater power
Threatened all. "Wait. Keep down. Some crack
May soon appear," said Little Wolf. "Attack
When they get close." Then soon he said, "Now fire,
My friends." Amazed, they saw the whites retire.

Why had not the soldiers pressed the kill?
Why not Sand Creek once again, or why
Not Sappa ways? These surely had the will
Of former foes. The Colonel soon might die,
They learned, so the cavalry withdrew to try
Another way. But in the deep of night
Wolf's battered folk raced miles away in flight.

The Cheyenne party held a northward path,
With seasoned soldiers waiting at the Platte
And bluecoats pressing from behind in wrath.
The band was fewer now, but heartened at
The sight of old familiar haunts—the flat
And hilly regions long so dear to all,
By now in clutch of frosty, yellow fall.

They crossed at Ogallala, out of sight
Of all, despite the thousand soldiers poised
Nearby. They moved, a long dark string in flight,
To White Tail Creek, and camped. With scouts deployed,
The Cheyenne Council let the word be noised
Abroad to friendly ears for news to guide
Them through the *vehos** yet to be defied.

The word was bad. Soldiers camped along
White River and the Red Cloud Agency.
And the Sioux, their friends, a thousand strong
Now under guard. The Council met to see
What could be done. Dull Knife voiced a plea
To stop. "These soldiers are our friends," he said.
"Unless we stop, we'll lose more lives ahead."

"The soldiers wish to catch and kill us all,"
Said Little Wolf. "You are a fool," the Knife
Replied. "The whites are not our friends. Recall
How much they've lied," said Wolf. "But we'll have life
Instead of daily deaths," said Knife. The strife
Between the two was bitter, and the chiefs
Led factions based on strongly charged beliefs.

The upshot was that Knife led half the camp
Away, surrendering in time to whites.
Again they were betrayed, and forced to tramp
Back south–except for dozens dead from fights
In hopeless, helpless rage. They had no rights
Despite a growing admiration in
The land for folk who fought so hard to win.

(**The Cheyenne word for white men.*)

Wolf's people meanwhile scattered to the hills
And hid until the scouts said all was clear.
They gathered in a valley then, their ills
Forgotten in the joy of peace. Their cheer
Was great, if tempered by great loss and fear
Of further molestation. Fish and deer
And ducks and other goods seemed bounties here.

They settled in, preparing robes and hides
From beef and deer. Wolf wished to winter here
And soon had everyone engaged. All sides
Of camp were watched lest enemies appear—
And passing days saw lessening of fear.
The peace and rest and plenty were enjoyed
As men and women found themselves employed.

The camp was small, one hundred twenty-six,
A third of those who left the southern plain
Some months before. They needed now to fix
Their minds on things ahead, and not on pain
And losses touching each. Wolf knew the strain
Of recent days would slowly ease if all
Could pull together for a common goal.

The soldiers searched for Little Wolf each day,
But never really threatened him at all,
For Cheyenne vigilance was kept in play.
The bitter winds caused temperatures to fall
So suffering increased for great and small.
Frostbite, ague, boredom, urgent need
Plagued the restive camp; they must proceed.

The Wolf well knew the tragedy of Knife.
Many witnesses to perfidy
Told how many were bereft of life,
Survivors sharing gross indignity.
But the lot was cast. Wolf had to see
His own folk safely to their northern goal.
They must not run upon a shoal.

Wolf's foragers moved out accordingly
For horses. Horses were a must. In days
The tribe were ready. They still hoped to see
The Yellowstone, return to all the ways
They knew and loved and lost. They could then raise
New lodges on the old foundations
And build new lives on age-old expectations.

They travelled slowly in newfallen snow
And shivered in the February chill.
They moved northwestward, ever on the go,
Stirred by passion and an iron will,
Armed with purpose, carried out with skill.
They came one day to their northern home
Determined they would stay—no longer roam.

Montana plains and wilds were welcome sights.
The weary travelers pushed on until
They reached a rocky rise, should further fights
With soldiers lie ahead. The chosen hill
Gave vantage to defenders who, with skill
Could force besieging men to pay a price
Beyond all reason, twice or even thrice.

Commander Clark of nearby Fort Keogh
Sent scouts to find the Wolf, and did. Clark came
At once to meet his former scout, no foe
If terms could be arranged. He pledged his name—
A trusted name—that he would make his aim
The peaceful settlement of Cheyenne folk
On lands so long their own. In faith, he spoke.

With trust, Wolf heard. He would not yield their arms
But led his band in friendship to the Post
Where food and housing waited. Further harms
Were possible he knew, but Clark was most
Reliable and true. Clark did not boast
His will could be achieved. He merely said
He'd do his best to have his wishes sped.

"The white man gives you nothing," Wolf had said,
"Until you hold it tightly in your hand."[1]
But this time fortune smiled. There were instead
Of calls for retribution in the land
A grudging admiration for the stand
The band had taken. Yes, there would be space
Assigned beside the Tongue for this hardy race.

The band had come almost two thousand miles
Through rugged country locked in winter's grip,
Through thousands of shooting soldiers, past the wiles
Of faithless *vehos*—a stirring, stunning trip
Inspired by Wolf's intrepid leadership.
All honor to the ones who made it through.
Such undying spirit is forever new.

[1]An American Epic, *Cheyenne Autumn*, Avon Books,
copyright 1953.

Cheyenne Indian Tepee

THE GERMAN FAMILY

John and Liddia German came west in an oxdrawn wagon with seven children: Rebecca (20), Stephen (19), Catherine (17), Joanna (15), Sophia (13), Julia (7), and Adelaide (5). They were attacked in Kansas by a band of hostile Cheyenne Indians on September 11, 1874, when five of the family were killed. Catherine suffered an arrow wound in her thigh, and was, with the three other girls, taken hostage. They suffered much from cold and hunger as captives, becoming very thin with fingers almost birdlike in their emaciation.

The girls were released by March of 1875. They were then adopted by Mr. and Mrs. Patrick Corney where they received loving care. They all grew up to marry and have families, surviving into the 1930's and 1940's at advanced age.

On September 9, 1990, one hundred fourteen German family descendants met with John Sipes, great-great grandson of Medicine Water, his family, and other Cheyennes to heal the memories. Perhaps five hundred spectators witnessed the peace making ceremony where the North Fork joins the Smoky Hill River, the site of the massacre.

A Frontier Fort

THE SMOKY HILL RIVER AFFAIR

John German dreamed of Colorado lands
For years before he took his family
And headed west. He'd heard of hostile bands
Of Indians, incensed that they must flee
Ancestral hunting grounds, but thought that he
Might make it through.

He drove with patience mile by mile, until
He neared Fort Wallace. There he camped one night,
As many nights before, quite near a hill
And deep ravine. He chose a level site
And settled down. Thin clouds subdued the light
Of moon and stars.

It was a night like any other night
Except that mid-September chilly air
Told of approaching fall. Then morning light
Dawned clear, arousing each to a practiced share
In daily chores, from children's needs to care
For animals.

The seven children shared their father's dream
Of homestead lands and open western spaces.
The vistas of their vision made it seem
They thought as one. They daily spoke of places
That they'd long since heard could be the basis
For new lives.

Rebecca was the eldest, Adelaide
But five. Stephen was the only son.
He shared guard duties every night and made
His mark each morning with his flintlock gun
When meat supplies ran low. The rising sun
Now summoned all.

The younger children dawdled as they dared,
The older girls all busy with the meal,
The fire, blankets, water, as they shared
In willing service with their mom. Each squeal
And giggle told how glad they were to feel
So near the fort.

Breakfast done, the wagon packed, Steve
And Catherine headed out to get the cow
And calf. The seven others took their leave
Of yet another camp, all eager now
To reach the fort, a place that would allow
Them rest from fear.

Then all at once the air was split with cries
And shouts as painted warriors raced on down
The hill before John's startled, frightened eyes.
The raid was swift and deadly. Soon the ground
was soaked with blood, the arid, dusty brown
Dark-stained with red.

The family were paralyzed with fear,
Yet struggled to defend themselves. One brave
Prepared to kill the tot because her tears
And cries annoyed him—but an early grave
Was cheated when a squaw jumped in to save
The hapless child.

Steve was shot and Catherine wounded, John
And Liddia killed. Rebecca too. Just four
Were left unhurt until Joanna's blond
Long hair became a prize too great t'ignore.
A brave killed her and left her in her gore.
The rest were spared.

Five Germans killed and scalped! The rest
Were taken captive and driven fast away.
They travelled night and day. The Indians pressed
On south and west. They knew they must not stay
Near cavalry—those whites would sure repay
Their deed in kind.

The nineteen Indians pressed ahead, then hid
Three days to watch for troops. A sudden fright,
However, caused the band to flee and rid
Themselves of Adelaide and Julie quite
Capriciously, a shocking desperate plight
For two young girls.

The two—five and seven years of age—
Were left unharmed to make their way alone
And hoped by following wagon tracks t'engage
A settler or a fort. They wandered on
Eating onions, grasses, berries, plums
A whole six weeks.

Medicine Water's band pushed on. They found
The Cheyenne camp and danced in triumph, glad
To let the trophies of their raid redound
To their grand coup. The older girls were sad
To learn the two were gone. They feared them dead
At Indian hands.

The Cheyenne then agreed to separate,
For smaller bands could hide more easily.
Grey Beard took Sophia. She'd await
His will and pleasure. He then planned to flee
Back north and east a bit, a refugee
From bluecoat wrath.

The young ones meantime hid, they suffered cold,
Until an Indian party found the two.
Chief Grey Beard took them then, and wished to hold
Them—with Sophia—in defiant view
Of mounting losses: hostages might do
What force could not.

The Indians remembered Sand Creek days
When Chivington attacked a peaceful camp
And slaughtered hundreds! So, if *veho* ways
Could be so cruel, why not seek to tramp
On whites, their lives for ours? Let us stamp
On them, they thought.

The German massacre was fresh revenge
For losses at Adobe Walls, when son
To Chieftain Stone Calf lost his life. T'avenge
These deaths and mutilations, patience gone,
The Indians in reckless anger won
Their blow for blow.

A hunter meanwhile found the sad remains—
Five bodies and a half-burned wagon. Near
At hand the family Bible lay. The names
And dates and places made it clear
The four girls had been forced to disappear
Against their will.

The army took it ill. General Miles
Set wheels in motion. Soon the word was out
That hostile Indians must be stopped. The trials
Plaguing settlers had to end. No doubt
Remained in any mind. He meant to rout
All renegades.

Miles sent a captain for supplies one day
Complete with soldiers and a long mule train
With orders to attack the foe if they
Appeared in force. Word from outposts came
That Grey Beard's camp was near. They might attain
The general's end.

The soldiers stormed the band with shot and shout,
Convinced the girls were there. The mules and crew
Raced through the camp. Confusion reigned. But out
Of chaos glad success: the younger two
Emerged unscathed, except half-starved and blue
From bitter cold.

But not Sophia. Grey Beard had her still
And kept her. Nelson Miles advanced. The cold
Of winter plagued the Indians. His will
Was firm, though gentle as he learned that old
And young were starving. Miles pressed on, while bold
Grey Beard held out.

Catherine was with Stone Calf. She was well
Again, though cold and hungry. Stone Calf tried
To pressure Beard, but nothing he could tell
His neighbor brought a change, until the tide
Of suffering folk arose so high he spied
No other way.

In March of eighteen seventy-five, the last
Two girls were freed. Wagonloads of food
And clothing were advanced to break the fast
Long suffered by the tribe. The deadly feud
At end, the girls were safe, their fortitude
A thrill to all.

The girls were met near Darlington, a post
That served Cheyennes, and brought by ambulance
To army care. The soldiers kept the host
Of Indians in check. No mischance
Must mar the peace secured at last, no dance
Of death ensue.

The six-month hostages were safe, returned
To white men's ways. But Cheyenne goals were met
As well. New treaties followed, largely earned
Through blood and suffering. In time they set
Their feet anew on lands their own—a debt
Too lately paid.

THE CHEROKEE STRIP

The Cherokee Strip (more accurately the Cherokee Outlet) was a tract of land that lay along the northern border of Oklahoma. It extended fifty-eight miles north and south, and two hundred twenty-six miles east to west (from the 96th to the 100th meridians). It contained 13,000,000 acres. On May 17, 1893, the Cherokee Indians sold the Strip to the federal government, and on September 16, 1893, the land was opened to settlers. The government had established registration booths for them at Arkansas City, Caldwell, Hunnewell and Kiowa on the north, and at Orlando, Hennessey, and Stillwater in the south. Prospective settlers were to register at one of these seven sites, then wait for a signal at high noon on the sixteenth before entering the land. A few who jumped the gun were killed.

People raced on almost everything—buckboards, surreys, carts, covered wagons, bicycles, ponies, thoroughbreds. Some walked. One stepped across the line and drove a stake. Two steam-powered trains, each with forty-two cattlecars, loaded outside and in, carried passengers into the Strip (rails had long since been laid).

The land was already surveyed and platted, with towns and other administrative plots marked. Army units had tried to clear the area of all potential settlers, so that each person would have a fair chance. But the area was so large that the few soldiers assigned to duty were insufficient to patrol it. Consequently some settlers—Sooners—slipped into the Strip early and hid, hoping to gain an advantage. Some were caught and denied the right to settle, but many succeeded.

The run of September 16, 1893, was the last of four such events.

The Cherokee Strip Run

THE RUN

What a day! One hundred thousand men
And women, horses, ponies, mules, and then
The buckboards, covered wagons, carts, and trains
All poised along the lines to race for claims
On lands the Cherokees had sold! So hot
And dry! They waited for the signal shot
To clear the gates, impatiently. Some folk
Had camped nearby for days, but as the stroke
Of noon approached, a thousand milling feet
Had ground the earth to dust. The drouth and heat
Combined to test a saint. Among the crowd
Was Johnny Bell, a lad who long had vowed
To beat all others to the promised land.
He drove a homemade cart pulled by a span
Of geldings, beasts as swift as hares in flight.
He eyed the cresting sun and knew the fight
For place would soon begin. The moment neared.
The people tensed as minutes fled, then cheered
And bolted as a shot rang out. Too soon!
A sergeant shouted "Stop! It isn't noon!"
He pulled his gun, but no one stopped. He shot,
And one man fell, but the surging crowd was not
About to heed. They charged in clouds of dust
Across the line. Young Johnny knew he must
Lead out or be run down. He flicked his whip
And moments later dashed into the Strip
At headlong pace. With wagons to the right
And ponies to the left, he raced in tight
Formation on the plain. Men soon fanned out,
And Johnny urged his lively team to rout
The competition. No such luck. He lost
The lead to horsemen on their mounts and crossed
Their tracks a dozen times before he chose
To follow three upon a trail that rose

Across a wooded hill. He followed close,
And on the other side cried out to let
Him pass. No word. Their jaded mounts were wet
With sweat, and flagging. "Let me pass," John cried
Again, when suddenly one broke its stride,
Collapsed, and sprawled across the trail. Too late
To stop, John held the team at furious gait.
They leaped across the fallen man and horse,
While John and the cart bounced high. He kept his course
Towards Enid and his claim while dust swirled high
To join the smoke ascending to the sky
From scattered prairie fires. Tinder dry,
The grass burst into flame with frightful ease—
A locomotive's spark fanned by the breeze,
A cigarette or match could cause a blaze
To dim the scorching sun. Yet eager men,
Despite the dust and smoke sought out again
And again the way to fortune. Sooners tried
To beat their game. Some hid in draws, then lied
About the race. One hid inside a tent
A postman dragged along the ground (He meant
To help his brother get there first). One tried
A soldier's uniform as ruse. They plied
A busy trade to cheat and win. But most
Were honest like young John. The gathered host
Observed the rules and struggled for a place.
One Charley staked a claim, when, in the race
A woman wept, "I've failed!" He said, "Take mine,"
And hurried on. He made another find,
And Charley settled on new range. John Bell
Remained near Enid where he lived to tell
His story to the grandkids, how he ran
The race and won his quarter, man-to-man.

WILLIAM C. QUANTRILL

William Quantrill was a Confederate leader of Missourians called Border Ruffians or Bushwackers. He led several guerrilla forays into Kansas in 1862 and again in 1863. His counterpart from Kansas was a faction known as Jayhawkers, or Redlegs, mostly led by James Lane. Each group engaged in bloody raids and destroyed towns and farms summarily in the course of the Civil War.

On August twentieth of 1863 Quantrill led a group of men, estimated from 300 to 400 in number, to Lawrence. They were not observed, and camped just east of town. At dawn on the twenty-first they descended on the city and killed men and boys indiscriminately. They trampled one group of Negro recruits camped in the center of town. By nine o'clock almost 150 men and boys lay dead, and thirty were wounded. Most of the city was in ruins. Quantrill then returned to the Missouri hills some fifty miles away, eluding all pursuit.

Lawrence in Flames

QUANTRILL'S RAID

August 21, 1863

I never will forget that day.
Those demons came at dawn with shout
And shot that roused the town which lay
In sleep—or had just come about.

They were from hell. They had to be,
For when, soon after noon, they left,
The town lay waste in flames, and we,
The women, wandered dazed, bereft.

Our men and boys lay dead, or dying,
Houses charred, or gone, or burning,
Daughters frightened, shocked, and crying,
Treasures looted, tempers churning.

The raiders started with the stores
Downtown, and Eldridge House, then learned
Jim Lane was at his home, his doors
Just blocks away. Their focus turned.

The horsemen hurried to Jim's lot,
In haste to catch that special prey—
That ragtag horde, that polyglot
Of border ruffians on their way

To do great mischief if they could.
Old Jim, a canny rascal too,
Heard the din and sought the wood
Behind his house to slip from view.

He left in nightshirt, feet unshod,
And hid awhile in corn nearby,
His wife detaining men inside. One clod
Came near, but Jim kept from his eye.

They burned his place, of course, like mine,
His furniture and gear, but wife
And daughters left untouched—a line
The raiders did not cross. The strife

Spread then—hardly strife, because
Our men were so outnumbered. Most
Just hid, or ran, or died, their cause
Quite hopeless from the first. The host

Proceeded then from room to room
To ferret out all males. They killed
Them wantonly. Men met their doom
With courage, fighting hard till stilled.

One woman put her husband in
A cart she covered high with clothes
And wheeled him out secure within
The sight of ten or twenty oafs.

One hid her husband in the house
And when the raiders torched the place
She got permission as the spouse
To rescue furniture. The space

Inside a rolled-up rug she filled
With him and dragged him safe outside.
A group of sturdy women, skilled
In guile, set out a man to hide

As best they could. They shaved him clean,
Then dressed him in a scarf and shift
And hovered round his chair. The scene
Convinced each hostile eye, and swift

The ruthless demons swept away.
They were demons. They surely were.
Who else—*what* else—would stoop to slay
A five-year-old, I ask you, Sir,

All dressed in darling soldier suit,
With bullet through his skull? I rage
At just the thought. What kind of brute
Could do the deed? What *is* this age?

Soon after noon they rode away
And left a smoking, ruined waste.
The charred remains and bodies lay
In mass confusion, devil placed.

I wandered in that blackened place,
The earthly replica of hell,
Afraid to see a neighbor's face,
Uncertain what to feel or tell.

One woman held a blackened skull.
Another burned her hands on bones,
As both sought solace in the lull
That now prevailed, and wept in moans.

I later learned what kind of men
Could be so soulless, fiends like Cole
And James and Younger, lawless then
And lawless soon beyond control.

Jim Lane and others gathered friends
And sought the army. All in vain.
They soon returned to pressing ends,
To grief and anger, loss and pain.

SAM PEPPARD

Sam Peppard arrived in Oskaloosa when the town was perhaps eighteen months old, and he set up his blacksmith shop. He saw many oxteams going west on the Oregon Trail, just to the north, or the Santa Fe Trail, just to the south. He made repairs on many Conestogas. The more he saw these travelers, the more he dreamed of going with them. But not by oxcart. He would go by wind power.

One day Sam began building his windwagon. It had tall wheels and a lightweight body. When it was completed, he tried it out, and it worked well. But he could not manage the craft alone. He needed help. As Celia Barker Lottridge tells the story, he had four aides. I have given him one.

When all was ready, Sam did depart for Denver and rolled swiftly when the wind blew. He camped when it didn't blow. He did race a group of Indians, and he did come within eighty miles of Denver. There his wagon was destroyed by a dust devil, a twister.

He returned to Oskaloosa where he married and had ten children, supporting them through his well established blacksmith shop.

PEPPARD'S FOLLY

When Oskaloosa's days were young,
Her houses sparse, her people few,
A youngster from a schooner swung
A bag of tools to earth then drew
Himself erect and made his way
To folks nearby. "Hello," he said.
"I'm Sam Peppard. I'd like to stay
And be your smith." He built a shed
And soon was shaping horseshoes, nails,
Plowshares, rims. His forge glowed red,
His anvil rang, he increased sales
And prospered as his patrons spread.

He loved the wind. It blew his hair
And whipped his shirt. The southwind blew,
The southwest too, as weather fair
Or foul came sweeping, swirling through.
One day Sam quit his forge at noon
And turned to timbers in his shop.
He sawed and planed and shaped, till soon
He had a tidy hull atop
A set of spindly, slender wheels.
His neighbors missed the ringing sound
Of hammer blows, of steel on steel,
And came to see, but leaving, frowned.

"Young Sam is mad," they said. "He's made
A ship like Old Man Noah, not
A lake or river nigh. His trade
Is off. He doesn't care a jot."
Sam didn't care. He had a dream
That ships could sail on waving grass
As fairly as at sea. "I seem
Quite odd," he thought, "but let that pass."

55

He stepped a mast, then set a sail
And formed a tiller too. At length
He stocked his vessel, sought the trail
To try the ship and test its strength.

The village laughed when Sam set out,
But the wagon rolled serene. He tacked
To left, he tacked to right, with shout
Of satisfaction. He only lacked
One thing, he thought; he needed aid
In navigation since he'd set
His heart on Denver. Sam there made
His mind up. Luke would travel yet.
Luke was helper in the shop
And long had hoped to ride the ship.
The asking done, no force could stop
The lad from sharing in the trip.

One thing remained: a proper gale.
It came, and Sam and Luke sailed through
A gently mocking crowd: "Your tail
Will droop ere Denver welcomes you."
The vessel surged through Flint Hills grass
Two days and more, then joined the trail
To Denver. Oxteams watched them pass
In shock as Samuel dipped his sail.

Windwagon Sam sailed swiftly on
When winds whipped through with power,
But when the winds grew still and calm
The pair made camp—to fret each hour.
Full-bellied sails piled mile on miles,
The oxteams fell behind. But when
His sail drooped loose, young Sam drew smiles
From teamsters passing him again.

One day the wind blew like a gale
And Sam flew like a bird. He passed
An oxtrain, whirled along the trail
'Til three young Indians, riding fast,
Appeared to race the strange machine.
They raced abreast for many a mile
Until the three veered from the scene,
Their mounts quite spent; Sam won in style.
And so it went full thirty days,
Six hundred miles of starts and stops,
Till Sam and Luke could see the haze
Of Denver's backdrop mountaintops.

Elated, Sam held to his course
When dead ahead, he spied a cloud
Of spinning dust. Some mighty force
Was driving through with roar as loud
As rolling thunder. Twisting round
And round, the winds picked up the craft
And carried it aloft as bound
On high when suddenly, the draft
Dropped Sam and Luke on hull and sail,
A heap of twisted steel and wood
Across the wheel ruts of the trail—
A disappointing end that could
Have crushed a lesser man. But Sam
Believed he'd proved his point. He knew
It could be done, and did. His name
Lives on, the while he gets his due.

RAILROADS

In July of 1860 the first five miles of railroad were opened in Kansas, running from Elwood to Wathena. From that modest beginning came the surprisingly extensive network of rails that came by the 1920's to represent over 11,000 miles of track, the high point of rail service in the state. Currently there are about 9000 miles of track in use.

River barges and steamboats were, of course, the first commercial means of transportation. Mule teams and ox teams followed as the many overland trails were opened. But it remained for railroads to provide adequate transportation services for agricultural and industrial interests. Towns were born and prospered along the steel "Nile River." Towns which failed to lure railroads to their borders usually disappeared or, if not, remained small. All political and economic leaders therefore early gave prime attention to locating and financing and building the roads. The impact of railroading on all facets of midwestern history is incalculable.

Number 124

SAGA IN STEAM

Sturdy ox and mule teams built the west
Until the iron horse came on the scene
With hissing steam and clattering wheels to test
The mettle of the beasts that reigned serene.

The teams ruled masters of the well known trails
(The Chisholm, Texas, and the Santa Fe,
The Oregon and Osage Trace) till rails
Of steel made clear a race was under way.

The issue never was in doubt. The old
Ways had to yield to new. The railroad lines
Soon stretched across the state and soon controlled
The flow of freight and passengers. The signs

Were clear. The Kansas and Pacific ran
Due west, the Katy to the south and east.
The Santa Fe and branch lines filled the span
And served the west as revenues increased.

The oxen and the mules gave way to steam
And steel but kept their places locally
On fortune's turning wheel. The steady stream
Of time assured the railroad's victory.

The roads were shoddy, built with lightning speed
As lines competed in their schemes to claim
Vast tracts of prairie land. The public need
Was incidental to their drive for gain.

The ties lay far apart on grassy ground,
At times, no ballast to control the bed.
The rails were light, the bridges low, and bound
To wash away when raging rivers spread.

In spite of all, the railroads prospered well.
They carried cattle, hides, and coal out east,
Then lumber, furniture, and steel to sell
Out west. Demand for products seldom ceased.

Fine coaches, even Pullman cars, increased
Each passing month. The tide of settlers rose
Until the land was largely sold and ceased
To lie just for the taking. Others chose

To swell the towns and cities all along
The new life-giving streams. The gleaming rails
Brought trade and travelers who seemed a throng
To those who settled on the open range and swales.

But troubles plagued the roads from day to day
As bison flocked in herds across the track.
When wailing whistles failed to clear the way,
A jet of steam sufficed to move them back.

The trains were sitting ducks for bandit raids
In narrow draws or faroff lonely places.
Outlaws like Al Spencer used blockades
To stop the train, then cleaned the riders' purses.

But worst of all, most railway men agree,
Were Indian raids on builders—or a train
Well filled with passengers and freight. They'd be
Quite ruthless with the workmen, in the main,

Because they knew the railroad spelled the end
Of all they had and loved. They burned and killed,
They robbed and wrecked, until they came to
comprehend
The whites were bent on settling where they willed.

In time the army and the local law
Established peace. The railroads built new rails,
Their cars and engines grew in size, they saw
Their lines crisscross the land on massive scales.

The companies competed ruthlessly
For rights of way and cut each other's throats
For bonds. They fought with rates, and shamelessly
Engaged in the plunder naked greed promotes.

Steam stayed supreme till diesels cut
Their way into the pie, and in a ten
Year span the oil consuming monsters shut
The door on early storied steam-bred men.

But time's pursuing hand had further things
In store as cars and trucks and airplanes came
To race with railroad's vested ways. The slings
Of fortune dealt a blow that made the runner lame.

The roads have since been ailing, limping on
With courage, for the race is still not won.
Quite recent signs suggest a modest gain—
The marathon as yet is far from done.

THE GOVERNOR'S WIFE

Charles Robinson was the first governor of Kansas. He became an agent of the Emigrant Aid Society of New England in 1854, and by 1855 was established in Lawrence as a driving force in making Kansas a free soil state.

Charles had married Sara, a New Englander, on October 30, 1851, daughter of a prominent Massachusetts lawyer. Her father saw to it that she received a good education (by the time she was twelve she was an excellent Latin scholar and read French and German fluently).

Sara had lots of grit and made the most of a difficult pioneer life, though she didn't like many things about the frontier. She took long vacation trips home to Massachusetts during the first several years, but her husband's election as first governor of Kansas likely changed many of her attitudes.

Her early dislike of Kansas is easily understood. The Robinson's first house was barely framed when the couple arrived in Lawrence, and the cold, the rain, and the wind were pitiless in their batterings. Some pro-slavers had even tried to demolish the beginnings of the house before they arrived.

Despite Sara's restlessness, she supported her husband energetically, and she helped families in sickness, childbirth, and disaster. She was a good housekeeeper and a generous hostess. And she loved the natural beauty of the region. In a book entitled *Kansas: Its Interior and Exterior Life*, based largely on daily journal entries, she exclaims again and again on the wonder of Kansas trees, flowers, topography, and such.

She was as committed to the free-soil position as her husband, and supported him fully. She outlived Charles by fifteen years, dying at age 84.

SARA ROBINSON

My Sara is as rare as Indian pearl.
She came with me to Lawrence, leaving home
And comfort for the rigors of these parts.
A cultured Eastern lady, used to ease
And city living, Sara hardly blinked
An eye at frontier hardships on these plains.
Our house was scarcely framed—the wind and rain
Came freely in, and rattlers sought the warmth
Of hearth and bedding more than once. Our trunks
And furniture squeezed us, yet visitors
And travelers found welcome at her hands.
She loved Mount Oread and reveled in
The pristine beauty all around. She wrote
Unendingly how glad she was to share
The natural wealth of Kansas every day.
She was my strength. When conflict bore me down,
I found in her a sturdy will to press
The free-soil issue on. When I was placed
In prison, Sara filled these shoes out East,
Securing funds while sharing news and views
On struggles, fraud, deceit, and lies that plagued
Us settlers in our uphill fight for right
In self-determination. Back West again,
She found a hundred ways to serve at home
And in the nearby homes of needy folk.
She tended sick, she heartened those whose spirits
Flagged, discouraged over violence
And loss. She found internal grace to meet
The challenge of external forces ranged
About us everywhere. She kept, like me,
A journal of events and thoughts that paints
A panorama of our lives those days.
The early years were hard on her, but strength
And purpose gave her courage to persist.

When I was vilified, she stood with me
And dared unwary malcontents to spew
The venom of their hate. They rarely did
When she was near. I am forever grateful
For her goodness, faithfulness, and love.

JAMES HENRY LANE

James Lane was born in Lawrenceburg, Indiana, on June 22, 1814, though he claimed to have been born in a dozen places—wherever suited his purpose at the moment. He was a colonel of the Third Regiment of Indiana Volunteers and served with General Taylor in the Mexican War. He was a congressman from Indiana for one term, but pretty well exhausted his political possibilities in Indiana by then.

He came to Kansas in 1855, ostensibly to support Stephen A. Douglas' attempt to gain the presidency on the strength of the Kansas-Nebraska bill. Lane was to gain Democratic support for Douglas by espousing the pro-slavery position. He failed, so he flipflopped to the Republican antislavery position and supported Lincoln. As events became more tense and bloody, Lane organized Free Soil marauding groups, men ill disciplined and ill managed. Discipline among such troops was almost non-existent. Yet Lane's charisma and amazing eloquence kept him at the highest levels of Free Soil political activity.

He was ambitious and played rough and ready political games. He hated Robinson, the governor-elect (and governor by 1861), but made a deal to support him for governor if in turn he would be supported as senator. Lane did become a United States Senator from Kansas, and became intimate with Lincoln. When Lincoln faced doubtful nomination for reelection in 1864, Lane was the pivotal force that secured it for him.

Lane was insatiable for power, land, and wealth. He quarreled with a neighbor, Gaius Jenkins, about a land claim and, in the course of time, shot Jenkins dead in cold blood. Investigation showed that Jenkins had a valid title, but Lane even then got authorities to cede the land to him rather than to the rightful heirs.

That action more than anything else destroyed his political future. On July 1, 1865, he put a pistol barrel in his mouth and shot himself. He lingered until July 11, when he died. He is buried in Lawrence where a plain white shaft marks his grave. It contains this epitaph: "His faults, which were many, may well find sepulture with his dust. His virtues are enshrined in the hearts of thousands all over Kansas who still revere his memory as their great leader, counselor, and friend."

SENATOR LANE

Old Jim was a rascal from the start.
He came for fame and fortune, but he chose
The easy way. No principle for him.
He shifted parties, used the shyster's art,
Courted power, bribed and blustered foes
And friends alike to gain his slightest whim.

He was a redleg ruffian. He loved to raid
Missouri, but his lawless thieves despoiled
The folks at home as well. The army brass
Despised him, yet ambition drove him, made
Him ruthless in his drive for fame. He toiled
For status, serving self without abash.

He lacked conviction in religion, not
To mention personal honor, public trust.
His politics were shameless, yet he drove
To highest office, served with Lincoln, got
Him re-elected, came to Kansas, thrust
A bullet into Jenkins as they strove.

His faults were many. Yet despite these flaws,
Despite his motivations, General Lane
Deserves a place in Kansas memory.
He served the state those bloody years, the cause
Of freedom on the scales, and helped to gain
For all alike our precious liberty.

JOHN JAMES INGALLS

John James Ingalls was born in Massachusetts on December 29, 1833, and graduated from Williams College in 1855. His valedictory address entitled "Mummy Life" included a scathing criticism of the faculty. The college held his diploma for ten years in response. He moved to Atchison, Kansas, in 1858, where he immediately became involved in politics. He participated in the Wyandotte Constitutional Convention in 1859 and while there suggested a sketch for the great seal of the State. Much of it was adopted (including the motto) by the convention, but his rather simple symbolism was considerably altered before the final design was approved. He was a member of the state senate of Kansas in 1862, representing Atchison, and later active as a military officer during the Civil War. In 1873 he was elected to the national Senate where he served continuously for the next eighteen years. During those years he wrote poetry, articles for magazines, and spoke commandingly at all kinds of public functions such as at the dedication of a statue of John Brown in 1878. He was not reelected to the Senate in 1891 because a series of national economic reversals—no fault of Ingalls—turned the electorate against him, their scapegoat. He then retired from public life and devoted his time to private affairs and occasional public addresses. Shortly before his death he moved to New Mexico with his beloved wife, Anna, where he died on August 16, 1900. On January 21, 1905, the Congress of the United States met bicamerally to eulogize Ingalls as its members dedicated a white Parian marble statue of the man in Statuary Hall of the Capitol Building in Washington, D.C. Each state is entitled to two such monuments in the Hall, but so far Kansas has placed just this one.

Senator Ingalls in Statuary Hall

SENATOR INGALLS

He stands in Statuary Hall,
A marble tribute to the man
Whose golden tongue moved to enthrall
The people of the state and land.

Keen satire and invective served
Him in debate; his piercing eye
And flow of liquid words unnerved
Opponents brash enough to try

To best him in an argument.
He shaped our constitution, coined
The motto of our state, then lent
His voice to issues long enjoined.

Demosthenes or Cicero
Were not more eloquent than he.
He charmed a friend or flayed a foe
With wit and words used brilliantly.

A Senator for eighteen years,
He ranked among the best. His mind
Was keen, his courage great, his peers
Convinced he lived to serve mankind.

Immortalized in stone, he stands
Mute symbol of the sovereign state
He daily strove with heart and hands
To shape in vision, then create.

JERRY SIMPSON

Jerry was born in Canada on March 31, 1842, to a father of Scotch ancestry and mother of Welsh and English ancestry. He early learned integrity, industry, and independence, and by his twelfth year was working for a neighbor, by his fourteenth serving on a Great Lakes steamer. He sailed the Great Lakes for twenty-three years, rising to the rank of Captain. But after marriage to Jane Cape, and the loss of a great freighter, he came to Kansas to plant seed and watch crops grow.

He was an avid reader always. He read all kinds of things, and remembered. His memory was remarkable.

After a brief time in northern Kansas, Jerry and Jane moved to Barber County near Medicine Lodge. There he became interested in politics. Upon reading Henry George's *Progress and Poverty*, he became a populist (in what was called The People's Party). He was twice elected to Congress and there distinguished himself. His humor, his wit, his sarcasm, his clear ideas, his brilliant delivery, his kindness and friendliness, combined with his devotion to his fellow man, led to his being revered by his colleagues in the House. Although he was vilified early in his public career, he gradually earned the respect and admiration of millions across the nation.

Jerry earned the title "sockless" during a campaign in 1890 against J. R. Hallowell, Republican candidate for Congress. A newspaper taunted Jerry as wearing no socks, ribbing him about his modest means, but Jerry didn't deny it; instead, he accused Hallowell of wearing silk hose. The electorate, stung by low prices and widespread financial stress, decided that the candidate who admitted his own poverty was their man. And the sobriquet stuck.

SOCKLESS JERRY SIMPSON

A man of the people.
Gentle, kind, devoted to justice
And fair play,
He fought the railroad octopus
And led the fight against oil barons
Long before the public was aroused.
Witty, confident, alert,
With more than a touch of blarney to his tongue,
He spoke for those who bear the burdens
Of the farm and shop.
Putting him in the best of company,
White called him "Sockless Socrates."
An honest, kindly man
Cut from the same cloth as Lincoln,
He kept the public trust
And left a legacy of honor
And democratic gain.
A single taxer and free trader,
He stood on principle
And did the People's Party proud.

ALFRED MOSSMAN LANDON

Alfred Landon was born in western Pennsylvania on September 9, 1887, and came to Kansas in 1904. His father, John Landon, had been called to be Superintendent of the Kansas Natural Gas Company in Independence and brought his family with him.

Alf entered Kansas University that fall and after graduation worked in a bank for three years before joining his father in the oil industry. He was a careful investor and manager in oil so that he became modestly wealthy over the long haul.

He was Republican, like his family, and by 1928 plunged into politics. He served in minor roles until in 1932 he ran for governor against two candidates, and won. One of his opponents was "Goat-gland" John Brinkley, a broadcaster who promised anything to everyone. Having won, Landon faced overwhelming problems caused by two converging forces: economic depression and drouth. The one exacerbated the other. Then in 1934 he was reelected. He cooperated with the New Deal the first few years, simultaneously curbing spending at all state levels. He cut many salaries, including his own. The result was that the state pulled through a most trying time and did so better than many others.

By 1936 Landon was nominated for president on the Republican ticket to run against Franklin D. Roosevelt. Landon had support from the Hearst newspapers, the *New York Times*, and other major papers, but lost decisively. He did not even carry his own state.

His chief gift as a politician, win or lose, was his ability to conciliate. That gift enabled him to create party unity time after time because he had a genuine interest in people and their problems. He was a good listener, and having listened, he sought to act on behalf of the common good.

Governor Landon lived in Topeka until his hundredth year. He is father to Senator Nancy Jo Kassebaum.

GOVERNOR LANDON

Superb helmsman of a battered ship
Making its way through ruinous rocks
As roaring winds and churning seas
Whipped the waves to a frothy foam,
Alf Landon steered the state on course
To harbor home. Depression woes
Plus drouth bedeviled leaders here
And everywhere, but Landon said:
"Don't have it? Don't spend it," and made it stick
Across the state. He was a friend
To all, conciliation his
Best means to unity and strength.
He steered valiantly among
The rocks and shoals the Finney pair,
The loss of jobs, the drouth, the reefs
Like goat-gland Brinkley—till his name
Was heard across the land as a man
Of destiny. He must bear
His party's standard as the one
Who knew the way, they said. His will,
Integrity, and folksy ways—
Plus balanced budgets—led his peers
To nominate him president
Of this great land. He had no chance.
He lost decisively, but kept
His hand in local politics
Until he was, in time, the dean
Of Kansas politicians.
A hundred years, he never lost
His wit, his humor, or his faith
In people and democracy.
He set a course and held it firm
Until the shoals were clear. At that,
He left the wheel to other hands
And went below to take his rest.

ZULA BENNINGTON GREENE

Zula was born in 1895 in Hickory County, Missouri, and moved with her parents to Kansas in 1910. The family lived in Chase County, near Cottonwood Falls, in the Flint Hills, where she met and married her science teacher and principal of the school, Willard Greene. There she began to write a weekly column for the *Chase County Leader*, but the editor felt that a heading "By Peggy" would be more folksy and inviting than "By Zula." That name, Zula tells us, was assigned to her by a romantic maiden aunt who found the name in a book she had read.

Her weekly output soon expanded to columns in fourteen weekly papers. By 1933, Zula and her family moved to Topeka, where she began writing a daily weekday column for the *Daily Capital*, now the *Capital-Journal*. She kept the name, "Peggy of the Flint Hills." She continued to meet deadlines for fifty years, retiring in 1983, something like 15,000 columns later. In 1983 Zula published a collection of favorite selections entitled *Skimming the Cream.*

During those years she compiled through her columns a social history of Kansas. She was also active in the Topeka Civic Theatre, doing whatever needed to be done: writing, acting, sewing costumes, and painting sets. She was a women's rights activist, though not a militant. She expressed her refreshing self through her dress—bright colors and flamboyant styles—and her pleasant, unpretentious manner. She never swerved from her natural, homey ways that endeared her to friends and to her readers.

Zula in Mid-Career

PEGGY OF THE FLINT HILLS

She skimmed the cream from every day
To fill each column that she wrote
With family tidbits, theater fare,
Neighbor doings, work and play . . .
With current headlines, men of note,
Women's interests, nature rare.

From 'thirty-three to 'eighty-three
She penned her feature for its place,
And readers knew just where to look
To find her wisdom, jab, or plea
For common sense. Her modest space
Surpassed the impact of a book!

Her twinkling eye and tousled hair,
Her uninhibited, friendly ways,
Her homespun wit and view of things
Combined with humor, verve to spare,
Suffused her columns all her days:
Her fifty years this tribute brings!

CHARLES SHELDON

Charles M. Sheldon came to Topeka in 1889 as pastor of Central Congregational Church, where he remained as pastor (except for a brief hiatus from 1912-1915) until his retirement in 1919. He preached a social gospel, yet held firmly to early traditional ideas on Christian behavior (no drinking, dancing, smoking, or attending the theater). He was generous, caring, tireless in ministry. When people would not attend his Sunday evening services, he devised sermon stories (like *In His Steps*) which he read aloud to his congregation chapter by chapter. The result was a full church each Sunday evening. Then he published the stories as novels.

The central theme of *In His Steps* is to remake the modern business world in response to the query, "What would Jesus do?" Thus all moral issues in contemporary life would be resolved by deciding a right course of action in terms of that question. Through a fluke, the book was not properly copyrighted on publication and Sheldon received very few royalties. On the other hand, because the book was in the public domain it was reprinted dozens of times—more than almost any other book except the Bible—including about twenty-five translations to other languages.

Sheldon was particularly concerned to help the 3000 blacks living in Tennesseetown, the ghetto in Topeka made up of those who had fled the south after the Civil War. There were clear racial lines in the city in the nineties, and he worked hard to improve the lot of these people. He and his church established a kindergarten for them, and, among other similar efforts, tried to find jobs for them. They were welcome in his church, though not many came.

He fought hard for Prohibition, and he agitated for "Christian" news. For one week in March of 1900, Sheldon, by invitation, edited the *Topeka Daily Capital* on the principle of "What Would Jesus Do?" It was a phenomenal short-term success: the *Capital's* usual circulation had been about 11,250, but during Sheldon's week it rose to 2,176,100 papers, worldwide. Why? Because his reputation as the author of *In His Steps* plus the use of youthful Christian Endeavor salespeople in England and America led to national and international orders.

Sheldon lived in Topeka until 1947, when he died in his eighty-eighth year. He was never wealthy, despite his fame. He was offered many handsome salaries to turn to writing and editing, but he was a pastor at heart. So he remained the Christian minister, travelling widely as lecturer and preacher.

CHARLES SHELDON

He burned with a steady flame through life
And, like a candle in its place,
Consumed himself the while his light
Shone clear. He preached of love, in strife
With envy, greed, and hate. His face
Against the wrong, he served the right
Each day.

He wondered "What would Jesus do?"
Then published *In His Steps* to share
A dream of what could be. He thought
To ban John Barleycorn, pursue
World peace, and called for news with care
That goodness, truth, and faith be taught
To all.

He was Saint Charles those early days
To many in Topeka. He
Stood for love of God and man,
And in that Gilded Age sought ways
To clothe the naked, feed the hungry,
House the homeless—"For we can,"
He said.

He thought all humankind are kin,
All equal in their need for school,
For work, for food and fuel. He tried
To help all people see past skin
And learn to live the golden rule—
All ghettos are the fruit of pride,
He knew.

But public men too often pay
A heavy price when children go
Awry—as Sheldon's did. He failed
His son. He served day after day
Away from home and could not know
The ache of loneliness that ailed
His child.

He burned with a steady flame each day
And, like a candle burning low,
Consumed himself in loving deeds
And words. He gave himself away
In selfless service, all aglow
With a vision how to meet the needs
Of all.

BIRGER SANDZEN

Sven Birger Sandzen was born in Sweden on February 5, 1871. In the course of his studies he spent several years in Stockholm with Anders Zorn, master artist, then with Aman-Jean in Paris. In 1894 Sandzen came to Bethany College in Lindsborg, Kansas, where he remained for the rest of his life teaching and creating lovely art, whether prints or paintings. He became internationally known and respected. He was offered many prestigious positions during the more than fifty years of service to Bethany, but he chose to remain in Lindsborg. He retired from teaching in 1941 and died on June 19, 1954.

Together with Carl J. Smalley, early promoter of Sandzen's work, Sandzen worked hard to encourage ordinary citizens to become interested in art. They did so by keeping prices low, conducting art fairs, and generally raising public awareness. The result is that hundreds of midwestern homes are today graced with the works of Sandzen and other regional artists. He has left an incalculable heritage in Lindsborg, and across the country, not least the well stocked gallery on the Bethany College campus committed to his work and memory.

VIBRANT SCENES

Poet-painter of the Midwest,
Sandzen fell in love with the Smoky River,
The Rocky Mountains, the Great Plains,
And spent his life telling their story.
They live in his prints and on his canvases.
They live in the vigor of each scene,
In the water that almost ripples as I watch,
In the mountains that speak to me of age and strength,
In the trees that invite me to their cooling shade,
In the canyons that echo back my voice:
I become a part of all I see.

FREDERIC REMINGTON

Frederic Remington was born on October 4, 1861, in Canton, New York. At fifteen he attended a military academy in Worcester, Massachusetts, and stayed there two years. Later he studied art at Yale and played football. These elements—love of conflict and the ability to draw—soon came together to prepare him for his life's work.

When he was twenty-one, Remington gained control of his patrimony and came to Peabody, Kansas, where he bought a sheep ranch. He was never a rancher. He hired help to do the chores while he himself sketched. He engaged in boisterous and carefree pranks in and around the small town to the extent that he was not welcome. But he learned a great deal about horses and people and the West, and sketched continuously.

In 1844 he moved to Kansas City, Missouri, where he bought interest in a saloon, but within a year the saloon changed quarters and Remington lost his investment. Fortunately, he had been painting and sketching constantly, and he was able to use these materials later on. Several happy breaks led to publishing drawings in *Harper's Weekly, St. Nicholas,* and *Outing,* and his illustrative career was seriously launched. After his initial move to Kansas, Remington returned to the East for his permanent residence. From there, over the years, he made multiple trips to Arizona, New Mexico, Montana, and Wyoming.

In 1893 he met Owen Wister, the leader in Old West story-telling, and the two began a collaboration which was mutually helpful. The two were very different in temperament and manner, but they struck sparks in and for each other.

The Bronco Buster by Remington

REMINGTON

He usually wrote to me, "My dear Wister,"
And for ten years we were colleagues.
I penned stories, and he drew.
Mostly.
Of course, we both struck out on our own.
He wrote stories—"articles" he called them—
And then made bronzes.
He worked clay and called it mud.
I tried my hand at poetry because
I could never draw a line.
Words were my strength.
So I kept writing. Mostly fiction.
His bronzes—the Bronco Buster,
Coming Through the Rye,
The Old Dragoons,
The Rattlesnake, The Savage,
Trooper of the Plains,
The Stampede—early upset me
Because they drove a wedge between us.
No longer did he draw and paint for my stories.
Oh, yes, he did. Some.
But we slowly went two ways.
We tried in art to do the same thing—to capture the Old West.
The West was really gone when we began in the Nineties,
But we didn't know it then.
We set out to capture the spirit of that West—
Its cowboys, its soldiers, its Indians.
We didn't pay much attention to squatters or nesters.
We lived the life, then told the stories.
Frederic sketched and painted,
And I wrote. I wrote about real Americans,
And Fred drew them. He chose action.
His drawings are dramatic.

He drew conflict—men breaking horses,
Whites and Indians fighting, scalping, shooting, racing,
Running, chasing, climbing.
Always action.
Only action.
He loved a scrap for its own sake,
And when he said, "Everything in the West is life,"
He meant struggle and violence.
He hated populism and quiet towns;
They spelled the end of the era which he loved,
And he refused to accept that change.
My *Virginian* and his *John Ermine* make the point
He left us too soon—at only forty-seven—
But his art is unsurpassed.
He caught the spirit of the Old West for all time.
I miss him and his rambunctious ways.

A LITERARY LIFE

Willa Cather moved with her family from Virginia to Nebraska in 1883, a girl of nine, first to Catherton but soon thereafter to Red Cloud, still the family seat. She was observant; she noticed everything, and she remembered. She cut her hair like a boy and took no interest in modishness. She went to the University of Nebraska, graduating in 1895, then on to a career in writing and editing magazines for the next twenty years, an apprenticeship something like Hemingway's. She was not interested in men or marriage. She had instead several close women friends, most notably Isabelle McClung Hambourg and Edith Lewis. Sarah Orne Jewett became a strong supportive influence in her artistic development. She wrote some poetry, many articles, and most notably, fine short stories. Her first novel *Alexander's Bridge* appeared in 1912, followed by eleven more. But it was not until Alfred Knopf became her publisher in 1920 that she became comfortably wealthy.

She kept in touch with her family in Red Cloud over the years as she moved from Pittsburg to New York and later to Jaffrey, New Hampshire, and as she traveled to Europe or the Southwest. She put Nebraska on the literary map, yet, when she died in 1947 she was buried in Jaffrey. Her simple white headstone bears these Wordsworthian words from *My Antonia*, "That is happiness; to be dissolved into something complete and great."

WILLA CATHER

She was a restless spirit,
Searching, probing for the truths
She found in robust lives
Transplanted to her red Nebraska plains
From storied Old World places—Sweden
Norway, Germany, Bohemia.
She found bedrock certainties
In Red Cloud
Along with fripperies and froth, of course,
Certainties as solid as the land itself,
And gave us Antonia, Thea,
Alexandra—even Anton Rosicky—
People as resilient and strong
As giants in the earth
Because they lived in harmony
With soil and animals,
With wind and rain and searing sun
As well as with their neighbors.
She gave herself to art,
As others to the Virgin,
And tried through clear and simple lines
To tell the old abiding truths
That, like the land, endure.

COLOPHON

Raymond S. Nelson, Ph.D., taught English for thirty-eight years at two institutions, Morningside College in Sioux City, Iowa, and Friends University in Wichita. He was named Professor of English, Emeritus, in 1990, and still continues to teach an occasional class at Friends. He has published four books of poetry: *Not by Bread Alone* (1982), *Reflections on Life: Birth to Death* (1987), *Tracings* (1989), and . . . *and the Kansas Wind Blows (1991)*.

The artist, Stan Nelson, is Dr. Nelson's son. He is a Museum Specialist at the National Museum of American History (Smithsonian) in Washington D.C. His specialty is type-casting, an important dimension to the history of printing.

The type face is Janson, printed on 60# Natural Nekoosa Opaque Offset paper.